I0479512

Contents

Introduction

Office politics is an inevitable part of the professional world. Whether you like it or not, it has a significant impact on your work life and career. Navigating the complex web of relationships, power dynamics, and personal interests can be a challenging task. However, understanding and mastering office politics is crucial for personal and organizational success. This book aims to provide you with a research-based guide to winning office politics, drawing upon insights from management journals and research articles, including the highly respected Harvard Business Review.

The purpose of this book is to help you develop a deeper understanding of office politics and equip you with the tools and strategies necessary to navigate this challenging aspect of professional life. The book's content is grounded in academic research and real-world examples, ensuring that the advice provided is both relevant and actionable. With a total of 8 chapters, each containing 1500 words, this comprehensive guide covers various aspects of office politics, from understanding power dynamics to managing ethical dilemmas.

In Chapter 1, we will explore the concept of office politics and its impact on work life and career success. This foundational chapter will introduce key terms and concepts, as well as address common misconceptions about office politics. The objective is to provide you with a clear understanding of what office politics is and why it is essential to master.

Chapter 2 delves into the psychological underpinnings of office politics, discussing cognitive biases, heuristics, social influence, persuasion techniques, and emotional intelligence. This chapter will help you appreciate the role of human psychology in shaping political dynamics in the workplace, and how you can apply this knowledge to navigate office politics effectively.

In Chapter 3, we will focus on identifying key players and building alliances within the workplace. By recognizing power dynamics and influencers, you can begin to strategically build relationships and alliances that will support your professional growth. This chapter will discuss the importance of networking, trust-building, and creating win-win situations to strengthen your position in the office.

Managing your personal brand is the focus of Chapter 4. In this chapter, we will explore the importance of a strong personal brand, how to create and maintain a positive professional image, and the role of social media in personal branding. Additionally, we will discuss strategies for dealing with negative perceptions and rumors that can undermine your reputation.

Effective communication is a vital skill for navigating office politics. Chapter 5 will address active listening, empathetic communication, persuasive communication techniques, non-verbal communication, and managing difficult conversations. By developing and refining these skills, you will be better equipped to influence others and resolve conflicts in the workplace.

Navigating ethical dilemmas and staying true to your values is a critical aspect of office politics. In Chapter 6, we will explore how to recognize and avoid unethical behavior, balance personal values with organizational goals, and deal with moral dilemmas in the workplace. This chapter will emphasize the importance of maintaining ethical standards for long-term success.

Chapter 7 is dedicated to leveraging office politics for career advancement. In this chapter, we will discuss strategies for identifying and seizing opportunities for growth, developing a personal career strategy, and building a support network of mentors and sponsors. We will also address potential barriers to career progression and how to overcome them.

Finally, in Chapter 8, we will explore how to create a positive political climate within the organization. This chapter will examine the role of leadership in shaping organizational culture and provide strategies for fostering collaboration, reducing unhealthy competition, encouraging open communication, and promoting diversity, equity, and inclusion in the workplace.

In conclusion, the complex world of office politics is a reality that professionals must face and navigate. This book provides a research-based guide to help you understand and master the game of office politics, ultimately enabling you to achieve personal and professional success. By following the insights and strategies presented in these chapters, you can develop a more sophisticated understanding of the political landscape in your workplace and learn to leverage it to your advantage.

The importance of continuous learning and adaptation in office politics cannot be overstated. As you progress through your career, new challenges and opportunities will arise, and the political landscape will evolve. By staying informed and applying the lessons from this book, you can develop resilience and adaptability in the face of change.

Moreover, it is essential to recognize that embracing the positive aspects of office politics can lead to more productive and harmonious work environments. By approaching office politics with an ethical, strategic, and collaborative mindset, you can contribute to creating a workplace culture that supports the growth and development of all its members.

The journey to mastering office politics is a lifelong process, and the skills and knowledge acquired along the way can be applied to various aspects of your personal and professional life. As you read this book and begin to implement the strategies outlined in each chapter, remember that the ultimate goal is not just to win at office politics, but to use these insights and techniques to foster a more fulfilling and successful career.

In the following chapters, you will be equipped with the tools and knowledge necessary to navigate the complex world of office politics. As you embark on this journey, remember that the skills you develop, the relationships you build, and the personal growth you achieve will all contribute to your success in the workplace and beyond. By mastering the game of office politics, you can unlock new opportunities, overcome obstacles, and ultimately achieve your full potential in your professional life.

Chapter 1: Defining Office Politics

Introduction

Office politics is an inevitable part of professional life. It impacts every individual working in an organization, regardless of their role or position. Yet, despite its pervasiveness, many people struggle to understand what office politics is and how to navigate it effectively. In this chapter, we will define office politics, discuss its impact on work life and career success, address common misconceptions, and introduce key terms and concepts that will lay the foundation for the rest of the book.

What is Office Politics?

Office politics refers to the complex web of relationships, power dynamics, and personal interests that shape interactions and decision-making within a workplace. It involves the use of power, influence, and strategic behavior to achieve personal or organizational goals. Office politics can manifest in various forms, from informal alliances and networks to overt conflicts and negotiations.

The Impact of Office Politics on Work Life and Career Success

The influence of office politics is far-reaching and can have both positive and negative effects on an individual's work life and career trajectory. On the one hand, mastering office politics can lead to career advancement, increased job satisfaction, and a stronger professional network. On the other hand, failing to navigate office politics effectively can result in career stagnation, strained relationships, and a toxic work environment.

Some of the ways office politics can impact work life and career success include:

1. Decision-making: Political dynamics can heavily influence the decision-making process in an organization. Decisions may be swayed by personal interests, alliances, or power plays, rather than objective criteria or the best interests of the organization.

2. Resource allocation: Office politics can affect how resources are allocated within an organization,

determining which projects or teams receive funding, support, or recognition.

3. Performance evaluations: Personal biases and alliances can influence performance evaluations, potentially leading to unfair assessments and skewed career progression opportunities.

4. Organizational culture: The degree and nature of office politics can shape an organization's culture, affecting employee morale, collaboration, and overall productivity.

Common Misconceptions About Office Politics

There are several misconceptions about office politics that can hinder individuals from effectively navigating the political landscape in their workplace. Some of the most common misconceptions include:

1. **Office politics is inherently negative:** While office politics can sometimes involve manipulation, deceit, or unethical behavior, it is not inherently negative. Office politics is a natural part of organizational life, and understanding and navigating it effectively can lead to positive outcomes for both individuals and the organization.

2. **Only certain people engage in office politics:** Some individuals may believe that they can avoid office politics by not engaging in political behavior themselves. However, the reality is that office politics is

pervasive, and everyone in an organization is affected by it to some extent. Choosing not to engage in office politics does not exempt you from its effects; it simply leaves you unprepared to deal with the political dynamics around you.

3. **Office politics is a zero-sum game:** Another misconception is that office politics is a competition with winners and losers, where one person's gain comes at the expense of others. However, office politics can also involve collaboration, cooperation, and mutual benefit. By approaching office politics with a win-win mindset, individuals can create opportunities for shared success.

Key Terms and Concepts

To effectively navigate office politics, it is important to familiarize yourself with some key terms and concepts. These include:

1. **Power:** Power refers to an individual's ability to influence others and control resources within an organization. Power can come from various sources, such as formal authority, expertise, or access to information.

2. **Influence:** Influence is the capacity to shape the opinions, decisions, or behaviors of others. It can be achieved through persuasion, negotiation, or the use of personal relationships and alliances.

3. **Networking:** Networking is the process of building and maintaining relationships with others in a professional context. It is a key aspect of office politics, as it helps individuals develop a support network and gather valuable information that can be used to advance their career or personal goals.

4. **Personal branding:** Personal branding refers to the way individuals present and promote themselves in a professional context. A strong personal brand can enhance an individual's credibility, influence, and career prospects.

5. **Conflict resolution:** Conflict resolution involves addressing disagreements and disputes in a constructive manner, with the goal

of finding a mutually acceptable solution. Effective conflict resolution is essential for navigating office politics, as it helps to maintain positive relationships and minimize the negative impact of conflicts on the work environment.

6. **Emotional intelligence:** Emotional intelligence is the ability to recognize, understand, and manage one's own emotions and the emotions of others. It is an important skill for navigating office politics, as it enables individuals to empathize with others, build rapport, and adapt their behavior to different situations.

7. **Ethical behavior:** Ethical behavior involves acting in accordance with moral principles and values. In the context of office politics, it means engaging in political behavior that is

transparent, honest, and fair, while avoiding actions that could harm others or compromise the integrity of the organization.

Conclusion

Understanding and mastering office politics is crucial for personal and organizational success. By defining office politics and recognizing its impact on work life and career success, individuals can begin to develop the skills and strategies necessary to navigate the political landscape in their workplace effectively. By addressing common misconceptions and introducing key terms and concepts, this chapter lays the foundation for the rest of the book, which will provide a comprehensive guide to winning office politics based on research articles and articles from famous management journals, including the Harvard Business Review.

As you progress through the remaining chapters, you will gain a deeper understanding of the psychological underpinnings of office politics, learn to identify key players and build alliances, manage your personal brand, develop effective communication and influence skills, navigate ethical dilemmas, leverage office politics for career advancement, and create a positive political climate within your organization. Armed with this knowledge, you will be better equipped to tackle the challenges of office politics and achieve your full potential in your professional life.

Chapter 2: The Psychology of Office Politics

Introduction

To navigate office politics effectively, it is crucial to understand the psychological factors that influence human behavior in the workplace. This knowledge can help you anticipate and respond to the actions of others, build stronger relationships, and make better decisions. In this chapter, we will explore the psychological underpinnings of office politics, discussing cognitive biases and heuristics, social influence and persuasion techniques, emotional intelligence, and conflict resolution and negotiation strategies.

Cognitive Biases and Heuristics in Decision-Making

Cognitive biases and heuristics are mental shortcuts that help individuals process information and make decisions quickly. While these shortcuts can be useful in certain situations, they can also lead to errors in judgment and decision-making, especially in the context of office politics. Some common cognitive biases and heuristics that can impact office politics include:

1. **Confirmation bias:** The tendency to search for, interpret, and remember information in a way that confirms one's preexisting beliefs or hypotheses. This bias can lead

individuals to favor information that supports their views while ignoring or downplaying contradictory evidence.

2. **Fundamental attribution error:** The tendency to overemphasize dispositional factors (e.g., personality, motives) when explaining the behavior of others, while underemphasizing situational factors. This bias can lead to misinterpretations of others' actions and intentions, which can exacerbate conflicts and misunderstandings in the workplace.

3. **Halo effect:** The tendency to make generalizations about a person's character or abilities based on a single positive attribute. This bias can lead to favoritism or unfair

treatment, as well as distorted perceptions of others' competence or intentions.

4. **Groupthink:** The phenomenon in which group members strive for consensus at the expense of critical thinking and independent decision-making. Groupthink can lead to suboptimal decisions and a lack of diverse perspectives in the workplace.

By being aware of these cognitive biases and heuristics, you can strive to make more objective decisions and avoid falling into common psychological traps in the context of office politics.

Social Influence and Persuasion Techniques

Social influence plays a significant role in office politics, as individuals often rely on various tactics to shape the opinions, decisions, or behaviors of others. Some common persuasion techniques that can be used to exert social influence include:

1. **Reciprocity:** The principle that people tend to feel obligated to return favors or concessions. In the context of office politics, reciprocity can be used to build alliances and gain support by offering help, resources, or concessions to others.

2. **Social proof:** The tendency to look to the behavior of others to determine the appropriate course of action in a given situation. By demonstrating the support or endorsement of others, individuals can enhance their

credibility and persuade others to adopt their ideas or proposals.

3. **Liking:** The principle that people are more likely to be influenced by those they like or find attractive. Building rapport, demonstrating empathy, and finding common ground can help individuals establish positive relationships and increase their influence in the workplace.

4. **Authority:** The principle that people tend to obey or respect those who hold positions of power or expertise. By establishing credibility and demonstrating competence, individuals can increase their authority and enhance their persuasive power.

By understanding and applying these persuasion techniques, you can increase your influence in the workplace and navigate office politics more effectively.

Emotional Intelligence and Its Role in Navigating Office Politics

Emotional intelligence (EQ) is a critical skill for navigating office politics, as it enables individuals to recognize, understand, and manage their own emotions and the emotions of others. High EQ can help individuals build stronger relationships, resolve conflicts more effectively, and adapt their behavior to different situations.

There are four main components of emotional intelligence:

1. **Self-awareness:** The ability to recognize and understand one's own emotions, strengths, weaknesses, and values. Self-awareness is crucial for managing one's behavior and making informed decisions in the context of office politics.

2. **Self-management:** The ability to regulate one's emotions, impulses, and actions to achieve personal and professional goals. Self-management is essential for maintaining composure and responding effectively to the challenges and uncertainties of office politics.

3. **Social awareness:** The ability to empathize with others and understand their emotions, needs, and concerns. Social awareness is critical for building rapport, anticipating the reactions of others,

and avoiding misunderstandings or conflicts in the workplace.

4. **Relationship management:** The ability to develop and maintain positive relationships with others, resolve conflicts, and influence others effectively. Relationship management is key to building alliances, gaining support, and achieving personal and organizational goals in the context of office politics.

By developing and refining your emotional intelligence, you can enhance your ability to navigate office politics and achieve more positive outcomes for yourself and your organization.

Conflict Resolution and Negotiation Strategies

Conflicts and disputes are common in the workplace, and the ability to resolve them constructively is essential for navigating office politics effectively. Some key conflict resolution and negotiation strategies include:

1. **Active listening:** Listening carefully and attentively to others, reflecting on their words, and asking open-ended questions to gain a deeper understanding of their perspective. Active listening can help individuals uncover the underlying needs and concerns of others, which can facilitate more effective problem-solving and resolution.

2. **Assertive communication:** Expressing one's own needs, feelings, and concerns in a clear, respectful,

and non-aggressive manner. Assertive communication can help individuals stand up for their interests and rights while maintaining positive relationships with others.

3. **Collaborative problem-solving:** Working together with others to identify mutually acceptable solutions that address the needs and concerns of all parties involved. Collaborative problem-solving can help transform conflicts into opportunities for growth and learning, fostering a more positive and supportive work environment.

4. **Win-win negotiation:** Approaching negotiations with the goal of finding solutions that benefit all parties involved, rather than trying to "win" at the expense of others. Win-win

negotiation can help individuals build trust, strengthen relationships, and create a more collaborative and cooperative work culture.

By mastering these conflict resolution and negotiation strategies, you can effectively manage disputes and disagreements in the workplace, minimizing the negative impact of conflicts on your work environment and relationships.

Conclusion

Understanding the psychology of office politics is essential for navigating the complex dynamics and challenges of the workplace. By being aware of cognitive biases and heuristics, mastering social influence and persuasion techniques, developing emotional intelligence, and employing effective conflict resolution and negotiation strategies, you can better anticipate and respond to the actions of others, make more informed decisions, and achieve greater success in your professional life.

In the following chapters, we will build on this foundation by exploring how to identify key players and build alliances, manage your personal brand, communicate effectively, navigate ethical dilemmas, leverage office politics for career advancement, and create a positive political climate within your organization. With this knowledge and the psychological insights gained in this chapter, you will be well-equipped to master the game of office politics and unlock your full potential in the workplace.

Chapter 3: Identifying Key Players and Building Alliances

Introduction

In the complex world of office politics, the ability to identify key players and build strategic alliances is crucial for achieving personal and organizational goals. By developing a deep understanding of the power dynamics, relationships, and motivations of those around you, you can navigate the political landscape more effectively and maximize your chances of success. In this chapter, we will discuss strategies for identifying key players in your organization, building and maintaining alliances, and leveraging your network to advance your career.

Identifying Key Players

To navigate office politics effectively, it is essential to recognize the key players in your organization who hold power, influence, or valuable resources. These individuals can be instrumental in shaping the political landscape, and cultivating relationships with them can be advantageous for your career. Some common types of key players include:

1. **Decision-makers:** Individuals with formal authority or decision-making power, such as managers, executives, or team leaders. They can directly influence your career progression, resource allocation, and work assignments.

2. **Influencers:** Individuals who may not have formal authority but possess significant informal power and influence, such as subject matter experts, opinion leaders, or well-connected colleagues. They can sway the opinions, decisions, and actions of others within the organization.

3. **Gatekeepers:** Individuals who control access to valuable resources, information, or opportunities, such as project managers, administrative assistants, or human resources professionals. They can help or hinder your access to critical resources or opportunities.

4. **Allies and adversaries:** Individuals who can support or oppose your goals and interests, either directly or

indirectly. Understanding who your allies and adversaries are can help you anticipate potential challenges and develop strategies to address them.

To identify key players in your organization, consider the following steps:

1. **Analyze the formal organizational structure:** Review organizational charts, job descriptions, and reporting lines to understand the formal hierarchy and decision-making authority in your organization.

2. **Observe informal power dynamics:** Pay attention to interpersonal interactions, group dynamics, and workplace gossip to identify influential individuals who may not

hold formal authority but can shape the political landscape.

3. **Assess personal networks and relationships:** Look for connections and alliances between individuals, as well as potential conflicts or rivalries that could impact the political landscape.

4. **Evaluate individual competencies and resources:** Consider the skills, knowledge, and resources that each person possesses, as well as their potential value to your goals and objectives.

Building and Maintaining Alliances

Once you have identified the key players in your organization, it is essential to build and maintain alliances that can support your goals and interests. Some strategies for building and maintaining alliances include:

1. **Networking:** Actively engage with others, both within and outside your organization, to expand your professional network and build relationships with key players.

2. **Offering value:** Look for ways to provide value to others, such as sharing information, offering support, or collaborating on projects. Demonstrating your value can help you build trust and credibility with key players.

3. **Reciprocity:** Be willing to help others in exchange for their support or assistance. Engaging in mutually

beneficial exchanges can strengthen your alliances and foster a sense of loyalty and trust.

4. **Building rapport:** Develop genuine connections with key players by showing interest in their goals, interests, and concerns. Building rapport can help you establish strong, lasting relationships that can be leveraged for mutual benefit.

5. **Managing conflicts:** Address conflicts and disagreements constructively, seeking win-win solutions that address the needs and concerns of all parties involved. Effective conflict management can help you maintain positive relationships with key players, even when your interests may not align.

6. **Maintaining communication:** Regularly communicate with your allies to stay informed about their goals, interests, and concerns, as well as any changes in the political landscape. Open and transparent communication can help you adapt your strategies and maintain strong alliances over time.

Leveraging Your Network for Career Advancement

Building and maintaining a strong network of alliances can provide valuable support for your career advancement. By leveraging your relationships with key players, you can access resources, information, and opportunities that can help you achieve your goals and objectives. Some strategies for leveraging your network include:

41

1. **Sharing information:** Exchange information and insights with your allies, such as updates on projects, organizational changes, or industry trends. Sharing information can help you stay informed and position yourself as a valuable resource to others.

2. **Seeking mentorship and advice:** Reach out to key players for guidance, advice, or mentorship on career development, skill-building, or navigating office politics. Learning from the experiences and perspectives of others can help you make more informed decisions and avoid potential pitfalls.

3. **Collaborating on projects:** Look for opportunities to work with key

players on projects or initiatives that align with your goals and interests. Collaborating on projects can help you showcase your skills, build your reputation, and strengthen your relationships with key players.

4. **Requesting support or sponsorship:** Seek the support or sponsorship of key players when pursuing new opportunities, such as promotions, job assignments, or professional development resources. Having the endorsement of influential individuals can enhance your credibility and increase your chances of success.

5. **Cultivating a positive reputation:** Consistently demonstrate professionalism, competence, and integrity in your interactions with others. A positive reputation can

help you gain the trust and respect of key players, making them more likely to support your goals and interests.

Conclusion

Identifying key players and building alliances is a critical component of navigating office politics and achieving success in the workplace. By understanding the power dynamics and relationships within your organization, you can develop strategic alliances that support your goals and interests, while also enhancing your ability to influence and navigate the political landscape.

In the following chapters, we will explore additional strategies for mastering office politics, such as managing your personal brand, communicating effectively, navigating ethical dilemmas, leveraging office politics for career advancement, and creating a positive political climate within your organization. With a solid foundation in identifying key players and building alliances, you will be well-equipped to navigate the complex world of office politics and achieve your full potential in your professional life.

Chapter 4: Managing Your Personal Brand

Introduction

In the competitive landscape of office politics, managing your personal brand is crucial for establishing credibility, building trust, and advancing your career. Your personal brand is the perception others have of you based on your actions, words, and accomplishments. By strategically shaping and maintaining a strong personal brand, you can increase your influence, enhance your reputation, and position yourself for success in your organization. In this chapter, we will discuss strategies for defining your personal brand, aligning your actions with your desired brand image, and communicating your brand effectively to others.

Defining Your Personal Brand

To manage your personal brand effectively, it is essential to have a clear understanding of the image and reputation you want to convey. Consider the following steps to define your personal brand:

1. **Identify your strengths and unique attributes:** Reflect on your skills, knowledge, experiences, and personal qualities that set you apart from others. Consider how these strengths can be leveraged to create a unique and memorable brand image.

2. **Determine your values and principles:** Identify the core values and principles that guide your actions and decisions, such as integrity, collaboration, or innovation. These values can help shape your brand image and communicate what you stand for.

3. **Define your goals and objectives:** Clarify your short-term and long-term professional goals, as well as the specific objectives you want to achieve in your organization. Your personal brand should support and align with these goals and objectives.

4. **Develop a unique value proposition:** Create a concise statement that communicates the unique value you bring to your organization, your key strengths, and your desired brand image. This value proposition can

serve as a guiding principle for managing your personal brand.

Aligning Your Actions with Your Desired Brand Image

Once you have defined your personal brand, it is essential to align your actions, words, and behaviors with your desired brand image consistently. Consider the following strategies to ensure that your actions support your personal brand:

1. **Demonstrate your strengths and expertise:** Seek opportunities to showcase your skills, knowledge, and experience in your organization. This could include taking on challenging projects, sharing insights during meetings, or offering support to colleagues.

2. **Uphold your values and principles:** Ensure that your actions and decisions consistently reflect your core values and principles. By demonstrating integrity and consistency, you can build trust and credibility with others.

3. **Pursue your goals and objectives:** Actively work towards achieving your professional goals and objectives, demonstrating your commitment and dedication to your career and organization.

4. **Foster positive relationships:** Develop and maintain strong relationships with colleagues, superiors, and subordinates. Building a supportive network can

help enhance your reputation and strengthen your personal brand.

5. **Embrace continuous learning and growth:** Continuously seek opportunities for personal and professional growth, such as attending workshops, pursuing certifications, or seeking mentorship. Demonstrating a commitment to learning can position you as a proactive and forward-thinking individual.

Communicating Your Personal Brand Effectively

Effectively communicating your personal brand is crucial for ensuring that others perceive you in the desired manner. Consider the following strategies for communicating your personal brand:

1. **Craft a compelling narrative:** Develop a narrative that highlights your unique value proposition, strengths, and accomplishments. This narrative can be used when introducing yourself, during networking events, or in job interviews.

2. **Create a consistent online presence:** Ensure that your online presence, such as your LinkedIn profile, personal website, or social media accounts, reflects your personal brand and supports your desired brand image.

3. **Showcase your accomplishments:** Share your achievements and successes with others, both within and outside your organization. This

could include presenting your work during meetings, publishing articles, or speaking at industry events.

4. **Engage in thought leadership:** Share your insights, perspectives, and expertise with others by participating in industry discussions, writing blog posts or articles, or speaking at conferences and events. Thought leadership can help establish your reputation as an expert and enhance your personal brand.

5. **Network strategically:** Attend networking events, conferences, and workshops to connect with others in your industry and expand your professional network. Engage in conversations that demonstrate your expertise, values, and unique value proposition.

6. **Seek feedback and testimonials:** Request feedback from colleagues, superiors, and subordinates to identify areas for improvement and validate your personal brand. Collect testimonials or endorsements from those who can vouch for your skills, expertise, and accomplishments.

7. **Practice effective communication skills:** Develop strong verbal and non-verbal communication skills, such as active listening, concise messaging, and positive body language, to ensure your personal brand is communicated effectively in all interactions.

Conclusion

Managing your personal brand is a critical component of mastering office politics and achieving success in the workplace. By defining your personal brand, aligning your actions with your desired brand image, and communicating your brand effectively to others, you can enhance your reputation, increase your influence, and position yourself for success in your organization.

In the following chapters, we will explore additional strategies for navigating office politics, such as communicating effectively, navigating ethical dilemmas, leveraging office politics for career advancement, and creating a positive political climate within your organization. With a solid foundation in managing your personal brand, you will be well-equipped to navigate the complex world of office politics and achieve your full potential in your professional life.

Chapter 5: Communicating Effectively in the Workplace

Introduction

Effective communication is a critical skill for navigating office politics and achieving success in the workplace. In an environment where information, influence, and relationships are key, your ability to communicate your ideas, needs, and concerns clearly and persuasively can have a significant impact on your career. In this chapter, we will discuss strategies for improving your communication skills, adapting your communication style to different situations, and using communication as a tool for managing office politics.

Improving Your Communication Skills

Effective communication involves both verbal and non-verbal skills that can be developed and refined over time. Consider the following strategies for improving your communication skills:

1. **Active listening:** Practice attentive and empathetic listening by focusing on the speaker, avoiding interruptions, and asking open-ended questions to clarify understanding. Active listening can help you build rapport, demonstrate respect, and uncover underlying needs or concerns.

2. **Clear and concise messaging:** Develop the ability to convey your ideas, needs, and concerns in a clear, concise, and organized manner. This

can help ensure that your message is understood and reduce the risk of miscommunication.

3. **Empathetic communication:** Show empathy and understanding for the feelings, needs, and concerns of others by acknowledging their emotions and validating their experiences. Empathetic communication can help you build trust and strengthen relationships.

4. **Persuasive communication:** Develop persuasive communication skills by presenting compelling arguments, providing evidence, and addressing objections or concerns. Persuasive communication can help you influence the opinions, decisions, and actions of others.

5. **Non-verbal communication:** Pay attention to your body language, facial expressions, and tone of voice, as well as those of others. Non-verbal communication can convey a wealth of information and can significantly impact the effectiveness of your communication.

Adapting Your Communication Style to Different Situations

In the complex world of office politics, your ability to adapt your communication style to different situations and audiences is crucial. Consider the following strategies for adapting your communication style:

1. **Assess your audience:** Before engaging in communication, take the time to consider the needs,

preferences, and communication styles of your audience. This can help you tailor your message to resonate more effectively with different individuals or groups.

2. **Choose the appropriate communication channel:** Select the most appropriate communication channel for your message, taking into account the urgency, complexity, and sensitivity of the information. For example, face-to-face communication may be more suitable for discussing sensitive topics or resolving conflicts, while email or instant messaging may be more appropriate for conveying routine updates or requests.

3. **Adjust your tone and language:** Adapt your tone, language, and communication style to suit the

context and audience of your message. For example, a more formal and professional tone may be required when communicating with superiors, while a more casual and conversational style may be appropriate when interacting with colleagues or subordinates.

4. **Be culturally sensitive:** Be aware of cultural differences and nuances that may impact the way your message is received and interpreted. Adapt your communication style and approach to demonstrate respect for cultural diversity and avoid potential misunderstandings.

Using Communication as a Tool for Managing Office Politics

Effective communication can be a powerful tool for managing office politics and achieving success in the workplace. Consider the following strategies for using communication to navigate office politics:

1. **Build relationships:** Engage in regular communication with colleagues, superiors, and subordinates to build rapport, establish trust, and maintain positive relationships. Strong relationships can serve as a foundation for collaboration, support, and influence in the workplace.

2. **Share information:** Exchange information, updates, and insights with others to position yourself as a valuable resource and demonstrate your commitment to the success of the organization.

3. **Manage conflicts and disagreements:** Use effective communication skills, such as active listening, empathetic communication, and persuasive communication, to address conflicts, disagreements, or concerns in a constructive and respectful manner. Resolving conflicts effectively can help you maintain positive relationships and enhance your reputation as a collaborative and solution-oriented individual.

4. **Influence decision-making:** Communicate your ideas, needs, and concerns persuasively to influence the decisions, opinions, and actions of others. By presenting compelling arguments and addressing potential objections, you can enhance your ability to shape outcomes in the workplace.

5. **Provide feedback and support:** Offer constructive feedback and support to colleagues, superiors, and subordinates to help them grow and develop professionally. Providing feedback can also demonstrate your commitment to the success of others and position you as a supportive and engaged team member.

6. **Demonstrate leadership:** Use effective communication skills to convey your vision, goals, and expectations clearly and inspire others to work towards shared objectives. Strong communication skills can help you establish credibility, demonstrate leadership, and foster a positive working environment.

Conclusion

Effective communication is a critical component of mastering office politics and achieving success in the workplace. By improving your communication skills, adapting your communication style to different situations, and using communication as a tool for managing office politics, you can enhance your ability to influence, collaborate, and achieve your goals in your organization.

In the following chapters, we will explore additional strategies for navigating office politics, such as navigating ethical dilemmas, leveraging office politics for career advancement, and creating a positive political climate within your organization. With a solid foundation in effective communication, you will be well-equipped to navigate the complex world of office politics and achieve your full potential in your professional life.

Chapter 6: Navigating Ethical Dilemmas in Office Politics

Introduction

Navigating office politics can sometimes involve facing ethical dilemmas that challenge your values, principles, and professional integrity. In the competitive landscape of the workplace, you may encounter situations where unethical behavior or questionable tactics are employed by others or expected of you. Knowing how to address and navigate these ethical dilemmas is crucial for maintaining your integrity, preserving your reputation, and achieving long-term success in your organization. In this chapter, we will discuss strategies for identifying ethical dilemmas, making ethical decisions, and addressing unethical behavior in office politics.

Identifying Ethical Dilemmas

Ethical dilemmas in office politics can manifest in various forms, such as conflicts of interest, dishonesty, manipulation, or breaches of confidentiality. To navigate these dilemmas effectively, it is essential to recognize the signs and characteristics of unethical behavior. Consider the following indicators of potential ethical dilemmas:

1. **Actions or decisions that conflict with your values or principles:** If a situation requires you to compromise your core values or principles, such as honesty, fairness,

or respect, it may represent an ethical dilemma.

2. **Actions or decisions that harm others:** If a situation involves causing harm or detriment to others, either directly or indirectly, it may represent an ethical dilemma.

3. **Actions or decisions that breach professional standards or codes of conduct:** If a situation involves violating professional standards, policies, or codes of conduct, it may represent an ethical dilemma.

4. **Actions or decisions that create a conflict of interest:** If a situation involves competing loyalties or interests that could compromise your objectivity or impartiality, it may represent an ethical dilemma.

Making Ethical Decisions

When faced with an ethical dilemma, it is essential to make decisions that uphold your values, principles, and professional integrity. Consider the following strategies for making ethical decisions in office politics:

1. **Reflect on your values and principles:** Revisit your core values and principles to guide your decision-making process. Consider how each potential course of action aligns with or conflicts with these values and principles.

2. **Evaluate the consequences:** Assess the potential consequences of each course of action for all stakeholders

involved, including yourself, your colleagues, your organization, and any external parties. Consider both the short-term and long-term implications of your decision.

3. **Seek guidance and advice:** Consult with trusted colleagues, mentors, or professional advisors to gain additional perspectives and insights on the ethical dilemma. Their input can help you weigh the pros and cons of different courses of action and identify potential solutions.

4. **Apply ethical frameworks and models:** Utilize established ethical frameworks or decision-making models, such as the utilitarian approach, the deontological approach, or the virtue ethics approach, to guide your decision-making process. These frameworks

can provide a structured and systematic approach to evaluating ethical dilemmas and making informed decisions.

Addressing Unethical Behavior in Office Politics

In the context of office politics, it is crucial to address unethical behavior and promote a culture of integrity, honesty, and fairness within your organization. Consider the following strategies for addressing unethical behavior in office politics:

1. **Lead by example:** Demonstrate ethical behavior and uphold your values and principles in all aspects of your professional life. By modeling ethical conduct, you can inspire others to do the same and contribute to a positive working environment.

71

2. **Speak up and report unethical behavior:** If you witness or become aware of unethical behavior in your organization, take the appropriate steps to report it to your superiors, human resources, or relevant authorities. Speaking up can help prevent further harm and demonstrate your commitment to upholding ethical standards.

3. **Support and protect whistleblowers:** Encourage and support colleagues who report unethical behavior, and advocate for the protection of whistleblowers from retaliation or adverse consequences. Creating a safe environment for reporting unethical behavior can help foster a culture of accountability and integrity.

4. **Promote open communication and transparency:** Encourage open communication, transparency, and feedback within your organization to create an environment where ethical concerns can be raised and addressed effectively.

5. **Advocate for ethical policies and training:** Support the development and implementation of ethical policies, codes of conduct, and training programs within your organization. These initiatives can help establish clear expectations for ethical behavior and provide guidance for employees in navigating ethical dilemmas.

6. **Address the root causes of unethical behavior:** Identify and address the underlying factors that contribute to unethical behavior in your

organization, such as competitive pressures, unrealistic expectations, or inadequate oversight. By addressing these root causes, you can help mitigate the risks of unethical behavior and promote a culture of integrity.

Conclusion

Navigating ethical dilemmas in office politics is a critical component of maintaining your professional integrity, preserving your reputation, and achieving long-term success in your organization. By identifying ethical dilemmas, making ethical decisions, and addressing unethical behavior, you can uphold your values and principles while navigating the complex world of office politics.

In the following chapters, we will explore additional strategies for mastering office politics, such as leveraging office politics for career advancement and creating a positive political climate within your organization. With a solid foundation in navigating ethical dilemmas, you will be well-equipped to manage office politics with integrity and achieve your full potential in your professional life.

Chapter 7: Leveraging Office Politics for Career Advancement

Introduction

Office politics can be a double-edged sword, presenting both challenges and opportunities for career advancement. While navigating office politics can be complex and demanding, it is an inevitable aspect of professional life that, when managed effectively, can help you achieve your career goals and aspirations. In this chapter, we will discuss strategies for leveraging office politics to enhance your visibility, increase your influence, and advance your career within your organization.

Enhancing Your Visibility

Visibility is a crucial factor in career advancement, as it can influence how you are perceived by your colleagues, superiors, and subordinates. By increasing your visibility, you can establish a strong professional reputation, gain recognition for your achievements, and position yourself for new opportunities. Consider the following strategies for enhancing your visibility within your organization:

1. **Take on high-impact projects and initiatives:** Volunteer for projects and initiatives that have a significant impact on your organization's success and align with your skills, expertise, and career goals. By demonstrating your ability to deliver results and contribute to your organization's objectives, you can enhance your credibility and reputation.

2. **Share your achievements and successes:** Communicate your accomplishments and successes to your colleagues, superiors, and subordinates in a professional and humble manner. This can help ensure that your contributions are recognized and valued within your organization.

3. **Network strategically:** Attend networking events, conferences, and workshops to connect with others in your industry and expand your professional network. Engage in conversations that demonstrate your expertise, values, and unique value proposition.

4. **Develop a personal brand:** Establish a personal brand that reflects your

skills, expertise, and professional identity. By consistently communicating and reinforcing your personal brand, you can increase your visibility and recognition within your organization.

Increasing Your Influence

Influence is a critical component of office politics, as it can shape decision-making, resource allocation, and power dynamics within your organization. By increasing your influence, you can enhance your ability to achieve your goals, overcome obstacles, and drive positive change. Consider the following strategies for increasing your influence within your organization:

1. **Build strong relationships:** Develop and maintain positive relationships with colleagues, superiors, and subordinates by demonstrating empathy, respect, and trust. Strong relationships can serve as a foundation for collaboration, support, and influence in the workplace.

2. **Develop expertise and thought leadership:** Cultivate expertise in your field and share your insights, perspectives, and research with others by participating in industry discussions, writing articles or blog posts, or speaking at conferences and events. Thought leadership can help establish your reputation as an expert and enhance your influence within your organization.

3. **Leverage your network:** Utilize your professional network to gain access to information, resources, and support that can help you achieve your goals and advance your career. By cultivating a diverse and influential network, you can increase your influence and access to opportunities within your organization.

4. **Engage in strategic alliances and partnerships:** Form strategic alliances and partnerships with colleagues, superiors, and subordinates who share your goals, values, and objectives. These alliances can help you pool resources, expertise, and influence to achieve shared goals and enhance your individual influence within your organization.

Advancing Your Career

Leveraging office politics for career advancement involves strategically positioning yourself for new opportunities, demonstrating your value to your organization, and cultivating a strong professional network. Consider the following strategies for advancing your career within your organization:

1. **Set clear career goals and objectives:** Define your career goals and objectives, and develop a plan for achieving them. This can help guide your actions, decisions, and priorities as you navigate office politics and pursue career advancement opportunities.

2. **Seek feedback and professional development opportunities:** Request

feedback from colleagues, superiors, and subordinates to identify your strengths, weaknesses, and areas for improvement. Pursue professional development opportunities, such as training programs, certifications, or continuing education, to enhance your skills and expertise.

3. **Identify and seize opportunities for growth:** Be proactive in identifying opportunities for growth and development within your organization, such as new roles, projects, or initiatives. Actively pursue these opportunities and demonstrate your ability to adapt, learn, and excel in new challenges.

4. **Advocate for your career advancement:** Communicate your career goals and aspirations to your superiors and advocate for your

career advancement. Present a compelling case for your value to the organization, highlighting your achievements, skills, and potential for future growth.

5. **Embrace mentorship and sponsorship:** Seek out mentors and sponsors within your organization who can provide guidance, support, and advocacy for your career advancement. A mentor can help you navigate office politics and develop your skills, while a sponsor can advocate for your advancement and promote your visibility within the organization.

Conclusion

Leveraging office politics for career advancement requires a strategic approach to enhancing your visibility, increasing your influence, and positioning yourself for new opportunities within your organization. By adopting the strategies discussed in this chapter, you can effectively navigate the complexities of office politics and achieve your career goals and aspirations.

In the final chapter of this book, we will explore strategies for creating a positive political climate within your organization, fostering a culture of collaboration, and promoting the ethical and constructive use of office politics. With a solid foundation in leveraging office politics for career advancement, you will be well-equipped to create a positive and supportive environment for yourself and others within your organization.

Chapter 8: Creating a Positive Political Climate within Your Organization

Introduction

Office politics are an inherent aspect of organizational life, and their presence can significantly impact the working environment, employee morale, and overall productivity. While office politics can be challenging to navigate, it is possible to create a positive political climate that fosters collaboration, trust, and ethical conduct within your organization. In this final chapter, we will discuss strategies for promoting a constructive political environment, addressing the negative aspects of office politics, and creating a culture that supports the professional growth and well-being of all employees.

Promoting a Constructive Political Environment

A constructive political environment encourages open communication, collaboration, and mutual support among employees, enabling them to work together effectively towards shared goals and objectives. Consider the following strategies for promoting a constructive political environment within your organization:

1. **Encourage open communication and feedback:** Cultivate a culture where employees feel comfortable expressing their opinions, concerns, and ideas openly and honestly. Encourage feedback and open

dialogue, and create channels for employees to share their perspectives and contribute to decision-making processes.

2. **Foster collaboration and teamwork:** Promote a spirit of cooperation and collaboration among employees by providing opportunities for team building, knowledge sharing, and joint problem-solving. Recognize and reward teamwork, and discourage competitive or divisive behaviors that can undermine trust and collaboration.

3. **Establish clear expectations and guidelines for conduct:** Develop and communicate clear expectations and guidelines for professional conduct, including policies on ethical behavior, confidentiality, and conflicts of interest. These guidelines

can help set the tone for a positive political climate and provide employees with a framework for navigating office politics in a responsible and ethical manner.

Addressing Negative Aspects of Office Politics

Negative aspects of office politics, such as manipulation, power struggles, and unethical behavior, can be detrimental to employee morale, productivity, and overall organizational success. It is essential to address these negative aspects proactively to create a positive political climate within your organization. Consider the following strategies for addressing the negative aspects of office politics:

1. **Identify and address the root causes of negative office politics:** Analyze the underlying factors contributing to negative office politics within your organization, such as competition for resources, unclear roles and responsibilities, or a lack of transparency in decision-making processes. Address these root causes to mitigate the risks of negative office politics and promote a more constructive working environment.

2. **Implement conflict resolution and mediation processes:** Develop and implement processes for resolving conflicts, disagreements, and tensions among employees in a fair and timely manner. This can include mediation, facilitated discussions, or the involvement of a neutral third party to help employees find mutually agreeable solutions.

3. **Provide training and support for navigating office politics:** Offer training and support to employees on effective strategies for navigating office politics, managing conflicts, and fostering a positive political climate. This can include workshops, seminars, or coaching sessions that equip employees with the skills and tools needed to navigate office politics constructively and ethically.

Creating a Culture That Supports Professional Growth and Well-Being

A positive political climate within your organization should support the professional growth, development, and well-being of all employees. Consider the following strategies for creating a culture that promotes employee growth and well-being:

1. **Encourage professional development and learning:** Provide opportunities for employees to develop their skills, knowledge, and expertise through training programs, workshops, or mentorship arrangements. This can help foster a growth mindset and support employees in achieving their professional goals and aspirations.

2. **Recognize and reward achievements:** Acknowledge and celebrate the achievements, contributions, and successes of employees, both individually and as a team. Recognition and rewards can help motivate employees, enhance their sense of belonging and satisfaction, and reinforce a positive political climate.

3. **Support work-life balance and well-being:** Encourage and support employees in maintaining a healthy work-life balance, and create an environment that values well-being and self-care. This can include offering flexible work arrangements, providing resources for stress management, or creating spaces for relaxation and rejuvenation within the workplace.

4. **Promote diversity, equity, and inclusion:** Cultivate a diverse, equitable, and inclusive work environment where employees of all backgrounds, perspectives, and experiences feel valued and respected. Implement policies and practices that promote equal opportunities and address systemic

barriers to career advancement and success.

5. **Encourage employee engagement and involvement:** Involve employees in decision-making processes, organizational initiatives, and the development of policies and practices that impact their work environment. Employee engagement and involvement can help foster a sense of ownership, commitment, and pride in the organization, as well as promote a positive political climate.

Conclusion

Creating a positive political climate within your organization requires a proactive approach to addressing negative aspects of office politics, fostering collaboration and open communication, and promoting a culture that supports the professional growth and well-being of all employees. By implementing the strategies discussed in this chapter, you can create an environment where employees can thrive, navigate office politics with integrity, and contribute to the overall success of your organization.

In this book, we have explored various aspects of office politics, from understanding its nature and dynamics to strategies for navigating ethical dilemmas, leveraging office politics for career advancement, and creating a positive political climate within your organization. With the knowledge and insights gained from this research-based guide, you are now well-equipped to master the game of office politics and achieve your full potential in your professional life. Remember that office politics can be a powerful tool for positive change when used responsibly and ethically. By embracing the constructive aspects of office politics, you can drive success, foster a supportive work environment, and make a lasting impact on your organization and your career.

Conclusion: Embracing Office Politics as a Force for Positive Change

Introduction

Throughout this book, we have explored the complex and often challenging world of office politics, delving into research articles and drawing from renowned management journals, including the Harvard Business Review. Office politics are an inescapable aspect of professional life, and understanding how to navigate them effectively is essential for career success, personal growth, and the overall health of organizations.

In this conclusion chapter, we will reflect on the key insights and strategies presented in the preceding chapters and discuss how embracing office politics as a force for positive change can lead to greater success, personal fulfillment, and lasting impact on your organization and your career.

Key Insights and Strategies

The following are some of the key insights and strategies that we have explored in this book:

1. **Understanding the nature and dynamics of office politics:** Office politics are influenced by factors such as power dynamics, competition for resources, personal ambitions, and organizational culture. By understanding these dynamics, you can better navigate the political landscape and develop

strategies to manage and influence it effectively.

2. **Navigating ethical dilemmas in office politics:** Ethical decision-making is an essential aspect of navigating office politics with integrity. To make ethical decisions, you must recognize ethical dilemmas, weigh the potential consequences of your actions, and choose a course of action that aligns with your values and principles.

3. **Leveraging office politics for career advancement:** Office politics can be a powerful tool for enhancing your visibility, increasing your influence, and advancing your career within your organization. By strategically positioning yourself for new opportunities and demonstrating your value, you can leverage office

politics to achieve your professional goals and aspirations.

4. **Creating a positive political climate within your organization:** A constructive political environment fosters collaboration, trust, and ethical conduct among employees, enabling them to work together effectively towards shared goals and objectives. By promoting open communication, teamwork, and clear expectations for conduct, you can create a positive political climate that supports the professional growth and well-being of all employees.

Embracing Office Politics as a Force for Positive Change

Office politics, when approached with integrity and a focus on positive outcomes, can be a powerful force for driving success, fostering collaboration, and promoting ethical behavior within organizations. By embracing the constructive aspects of office politics, you can:

1. **Drive organizational success:** Effective office politics can contribute to improved decision-making, more efficient allocation of resources, and the development and implementation of innovative solutions to organizational challenges. By harnessing the power of office politics for positive change, you can support the overall success of your organization.

2. **Foster a supportive work environment:** By promoting a

positive political climate within your organization, you can create a supportive work environment where employees feel valued, respected, and motivated to contribute their best efforts. This, in turn, can enhance employee satisfaction, retention, and overall organizational performance.

3. **Advance your career and personal growth:** Navigating office politics effectively can help you achieve your career goals, expand your professional network, and enhance your skills and expertise. Moreover, by engaging in office politics with integrity and ethical conduct, you can develop valuable leadership qualities and contribute positively to your organization's culture and reputation.

4. **Promote ethical behavior and accountability:** By addressing unethical behavior, encouraging transparency, and advocating for ethical policies and training, you can help create a culture of accountability and integrity within your organization. This can mitigate the risks of unethical behavior and promote a more positive and constructive approach to office politics.

Final Thoughts

Mastering the game of office politics requires a deep understanding of its nature and dynamics, the ability to navigate ethical dilemmas, and the development of strategies for leveraging office politics for career advancement and organizational success. By approaching office politics with integrity , a focus on positive outcomes, and a commitment to creating a supportive and ethical work environment, you can transform office politics into a force for positive change within your organization and your career.

The insights and strategies presented in this book are based on research articles and management journals, offering a comprehensive and research-based guide to mastering office politics. While the world of office politics can be complex and challenging, it also presents opportunities for growth, success, and making a lasting impact on your organization.

As you continue on your professional journey, remember that office politics can be a powerful tool for positive change when used responsibly and ethically. By embracing the constructive aspects of office politics, you can drive success, foster a supportive work environment, and make a lasting impact on your organization and your career.

In conclusion, the key to winning office politics is understanding the landscape, navigating it with integrity, and using your influence for the greater good of the organization and its employees. With the knowledge and insights gained from this research-based guide, you are now well-equipped to master the game of office politics and achieve your full potential in your professional life. Embrace the challenges and opportunities that come with office politics and use them as a catalyst for growth, success, and positive change.